DECLARATION

•

I hereby declare that
all the paper produced by Cartiere del Garda S.p.A.
in its Riva del Garda mill is manufactured completely
<u>Acid-free and Wood-free</u>

Dr. Alois Lueftinger
Managing Director and General Manager
Cartiere del Garda S.p.A.

OPERATION EARTH

PEOPLE TRAP

by
Dennis Leggett
and
Jeremy Leggett

MARSHALL CAVENDISH CORPORATION
NEW YORK – TORONTO

Library Edition Published 1991
Published by Marshall Cavendish Corporation
2415 Jerusalem Avenue, North Bellmore, NY 11710
Devised and produced by The Templar Company plc
Pippbrook Mill, London Road, Dorking, Surrey RH4 1JE

Editors: Wendy Madgwick, Steve Parker
Designer: Jane Hunt
Illustrator: Rod Ferring

Color separations by Positive Colour Ltd, Maldon, Essex
Printed and bound by L.E.G.O., Vicenza, Italy

Library of Congress Cataloging-in-Publication Data

Leggett, Dennis
People trap / by Dennis Leggett and Jeremy Leggett. – Library ed.
p. cm. – (Operation Earth)
Includes index.
Summary: Examines the historical and contemporary causes of world
overpopulation and reviews some of the difficulties in dealing with the problem.
ISBN 1-85435-378-0
1. Population – Juvenile literature.
2. Population policy – Juvenile literature. [1. Population.]
I. Leggett, Jeremy K. II. Title. III. Series.
HB883.L45   1991   90-46400
304.6 – dc20   CIP AC

Whilst the contents of this book are believed to be correct at the time of going to
press, changes may have occurred since that time or will occur during
the currency of this book.

Photographic credits
t = top, b = bottom, l = left, r = right
Cover: Zefa; inset: Zefa;
page 6 Zefa; page 7 Rick Weyerhaeuser/WWF; page 10 Ron Girling/
Panos Pictures; page 11 Mary Evans; page 12 B. Klass/Panos Pictures;
page 14 John and Jenny Hubley; page 15 J. Delorme/Panos Pictures;
page 17 Mary Evans; page 19 Sally and Richard Greenhill;
page 22 K. Morrison/South American Pictures; page 23 M. Freeman/Bruce
Coleman; page 24 Trygve Bølstad/Panos Pictures; page 26 Trygve Bølstad/Panos
Pictures; page 28 Mary Evans; page 29 John and Penny Hubley; page 30 Tony
Morrison; page 32 Hank Morgan/Science Photo Library; page 33 Alex
Bartel/Science Photo Library; page 35 C. B. Frith/Bruce Coleman; page 37 J.
Hartley/Panos Pictures; page 39 t M. Boulton/Bruce Coleman; page 39 b John
and Jenny Hubley; page 40 P. Harrison/Panos Pictures.

CONTENTS

ONE TOO MANY?

In Northern Canada, the snowshoe hare is the main food of the lynx. Plants are the food of the snowshoe hare. Scientists studied and counted these animals for many years. They found that when the hare population went up, a year or so later the number of lynx also rose. The hare population reached a peak over a few years, and the lynx followed. Then both populations fell back to lower levels over the following few years. This cycle repeated itself every five to seven years.

The simple conclusion was that the numbers of predators – the lynx – depended on the numbers of their prey, the snowshoe hares. Fewer prey mean fewer predators.

Nature works the other way round, too. Remove the predators and the prey numbers rise. For many years,

A RISING TIDE?

The population of the world has increased rapidly in the past 100 years and is still rising. In 1989 almost 16,000 births were recorded every hour throughout the world. This added about 385,000 people to our planet every day, leading to a population growth of almost 93 million in that one year alone. As the population rises, the demand for food, land, and energy increases. This in turn leads to more pollution and other major environmental problems.

people hunted mule deer on the Kaibab Plateau, Arizona. By the time the hunting was stopped, the deer's natural predators – such as pumas and coyotes – had also been killed off by people. The remaining mule deer, with no predators to control their numbers, multiplied. Within a few years there were 10 times as many deer.

Then the deer's food ran out. They had eaten almost all of the plants, leaving hardly any to grow again. In the two worst years, three-fifths of young deer died. Their numbers fell from about 100,000 to less than 15,000. This is known as a population crash.

Some people think that we humans are becoming too numerous for the Earth to support. There are about 2.5 times as many people today as there were in 1950. Like the deer on the Kaibab Plateau, there must come a point when there are simply too many of us. Will the human population crash, like the deer? Or will it go up and down in small cycles, like the lynx?

This book explains how the world's human population has changed in the past. It examines the reasons for the tremendous surge in our numbers in the present. It also looks at what might happen in the future – especially if we fail to control our numbers.

BREEDING SLOWER OR FASTER

*In nature, some animals can change their **breeding rate** according to the circumstances. One example is the African elephant (see below). When numbers are low, the females begin to produce young when they are only 11 or 12 years old. They have a baby about every four years. When elephant numbers are high, females may be as old as 18 years before they have their first baby. Then they have young every seven years. Could we humans be like the elephants, and change our breeding rate?*

A RISING POPULATION

Throughout history, there have been times when the numbers of a certain animal or plant have increased very fast indeed. This is known as a population explosion. It happened when rabbits were first taken to Australia, and red deer to New Zealand. It is happening now to humans all over the Earth.

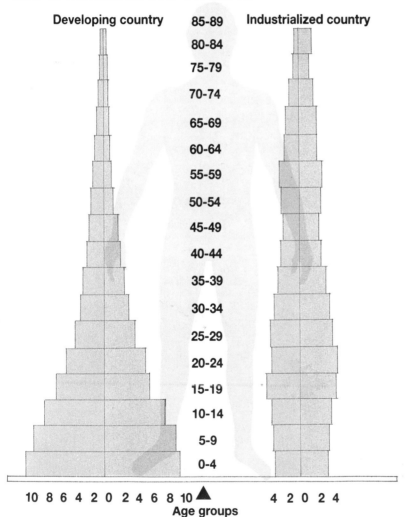

Developing country — Industrialized country

Age groups: 85-89, 80-84, 75-79, 70-74, 65-69, 60-64, 55-59, 50-54, 45-49, 40-44, 35-39, 30-34, 25-29, 20-24, 15-19, 10-14, 5-9, 0-4

10 8 6 4 2 0 2 4 6 8 10 ▲ 4 2 0 2 4

Age groups in years

% of population — % of population

THE POPULATION PYRAMID
We can draw a diagram for a population showing how many people there are in each age group. Pyramids for many poorer, developing countries are like the one shown here. Its wide base shows that their populations are mainly young. Its shallow-sloping sides show that many babies and children die. In richer, industrialized countries, the pyramid is much narrower and steeper.

□ male   □ female

8

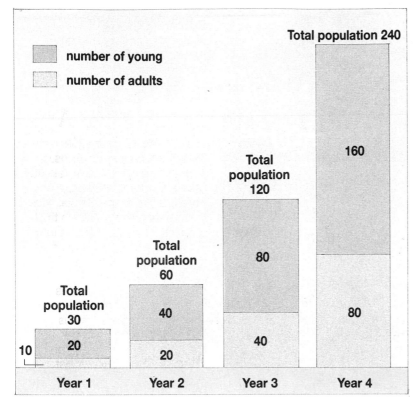

Total population 240

160

Total population 120

80

Total population 60

40

Total population 30

20

10

20

40

80

20

| Year 1 | Year 2 | Year 3 | Year 4 |

Australian farmers had no doubt that the numbers of rabbits were rocketing when they saw their crops and grazing land devastated. To study and understand in detail how populations of living things rise and fall, we have to count and measure them. If we count the numbers of the animal or plant each year for many years, we can see the way the population grows or shrinks.

Counting animals that live for one year and then die is easy. For long-lived animals, such as ourselves, it is more difficult to calculate. In human populations we need to know how many people there are in each age group, how many children each woman is likely to have during her lifetime, and how many people die each year, and at what age.

Demographers are experts who study populations. They do a regular count called a **census**. Using the information, they can provide us with a "population picture" which shows how long we are likely to live. This varies around the world. In many developing countries, babies and children are more likely to die young than those in industrialized countries. People in these poorer countries are unlikely to live as long as those in richer, more developed countries.

KNOW YOUR TERMS

People who study populations use various terms. We use some of them in this book.
● The number born each year compared with the total population is the **birth rate** or natality rate.
● The number dying each year compared with the total population is the **death rate** or mortality rate.
● Knowing the numbers that are born or die each year allows us to figure the rate at which the population is growing or decreasing. This is the rate of population change. If the birth rate is bigger than the mortality rate, the population grows.
● The average age to which people live is called the life expectancy.

PEOPLE IN THE PAST

The first human beings survived by hunting animals and gathering fruits, berries, roots, and leaves. Some Australian aboriginals still live this way, which is called the hunter–gatherer way of life. Then, about 10,000 years ago, people began to grow a few crops and keep animals. A small area of trees was slashed down and burned. Crops were grown for a year or two on the cleared land, and animals grazed there. Then, as the soil lost its goodness, the people moved on. A fresh area was chosen and cleared, while the soil in the old area was left to recover. This lifestyle is called slash-and-burn. Some Amazonian Indians still live like this, but their way of life is threatened by the destruction of the tropical forests.

Another way of life was to herd animals and move them to fresh grazing as the seasons changed. The Lapps in northern Scandinavia and the Bakhtiari people of Iran's Zagros Mountains have a nomadic history.

ROMAN RECORDS

The Romans were especially thorough with their records. They kept lists and catalogues of citizens and goods. In AD 79, the Roman city of Pompeii was suddenly overcome by volcanic gases and ashes when nearby Mount Vesuvius erupted. More than 2,000 people were killed. In the past 200 years, a clear picture of their daily lives has been excavated from the ruins. Here is the front of a Roman "fast-food" shop (see right).

DESERT LANDS

In the past, fertile lands have become deserts due to changes in climate or the activities of people. Today, some savanna grasslands and tropical forests are being ploughed up to grow crops or graze cattle or goats (see below). The land is often unsuitable and, without plant roots to bind the soil together, the soil dries up. The topsoil is blown or washed away, resulting in barren desert.

THE GROWTH OF THE HUMAN WORLD POPULATION

This graph shows how the numbers of people on the Earth have slowly increased over the centuries. It can never be accurate. Probably there were other peaks and dips, for example, when the Iron Age followed the Bronze Age, and when the Black Death struck in Asia before being brought to Europe.

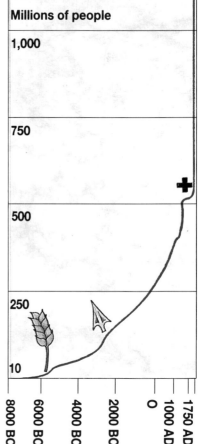

A few thousand years ago, people developed much better crops, especially wheat. They stopped wandering and became farmers. Wheat was a rich food and more people could survive on a certain area of land. **Civilizations** developed. From the ruins of their towns and cities, and from their records, we can estimate the numbers of people alive then.

People learned how to grow more food from the land to feed more people. However, natural events, diseases, and ignorance still dealt nasty shocks. The rich Roman farmlands of North Africa have become desert. The plague disease known as the Black Death, 650 years ago, killed up to one-half of the people of England within two years. When Europeans arrived in the Americas, they brought unfamiliar diseases which killed millions of people already living there. There were many other examples of disasters, but the world population slowly rose until around 1700. Then there was a change, as you can see on the next page.

Wheat developed
Farmers settle and towns grow up

Bronze invented, tools can be resharpened

 The Black Death strikes in Europe

11

A POPULATION ROCKET

Around the year 1750, a population rocket was set off. You can see from its smoke trail how our numbers have soared sky-high. The population rocket is powered by both the rich, industrialized and the poor, developing countries. At present, the numbers of people are rising fastest in developing countries. They are making the rocket climb steeply. Population growth in industrialized countries is not so fast.

The rocket's flight path cannot be foreseen accurately. Its course has been mapped from the size of the world population at different times. This information involves some guesswork, however. Not

BIG NUMBERS
Counting populations involves large, often confusing, numbers.

● One million equals 1,000,000 or one thousand thousand.

● One billion equals 1,000 million, or 1,000,000,000.

● One trillion equals one million million, or 1,000 billion, or 1,000,000,000,000.

● The world's human population today is 5,500 million, which is the same as 5.5 billion, or 5,500,000,000.

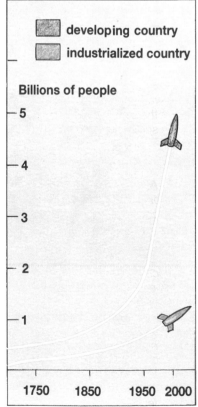

developing country

industrialized country

Billions of people

5

4

3

2

1

1750   1850   1950 2000

TWO ROCKETS COMPARED

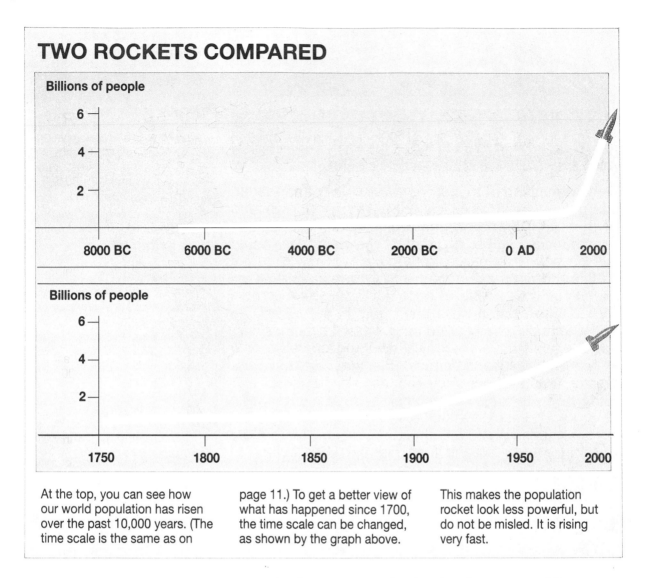

Billions of people

6					
4					
2					

8000 BC   6000 BC   4000 BC   2000 BC   0 AD   2000

Billions of people

6
4
2

1750   1800   1850   1900   1950   2000

At the top, you can see how our world population has risen over the past 10,000 years. (The time scale is the same as on page 11.) To get a better view of what has happened since 1700, the time scale can be changed, as shown by the graph above. This makes the population rocket look less powerful, but do not be misled. It is rising very fast.

MORE AND MORE PEOPLE

The populations of the world's poorer countries are going up very quickly. They have risen by more than 3 billion in the past 100 years. In contrast, the number of people in the rich, industrialized countries has gone up by about 600 million over the same time.

Many developing countries cannot afford to support their increasing populations. The people are becoming even poorer, with more and more living in slums and shanty towns like this one in Bangladesh (see left).

even the best census is absolutely correct. Allowances must be made for mistakes in the information collected.

In countries such as the United States, Britain, and Australia, gathering census information is relatively easy. Most people have an address, most can read and write, and there is regular postage and transportation. In other countries, people may be crowded in huge cities without anywhere to live, or they might be wandering over vast areas where there are hardly any roads or towns. Many people may not be able to read and write.

The United Nations, which forecasts populations in the future, must make allowances for this. It predicts what might happen by giving "high" and "low" paths which the population rocket might follow.

NO PREDATORS?

At the beginning of this book, you saw what happened when mule deer were left unhunted by pumas and coyotes (and humans). The recent human population increase looks rather like that of the deer. We should ask: Have we escaped our predators?

We are now threatened mainly by ourselves. We are the only animal willing to hunt down and kill our own kind. Warfare has always been part of our history. In recent times we have killed each other by the millions, and we even have the power to wipe ourselves out entirely with nuclear weapons. Even so, wars have not directly stopped our meteoric rise in numbers. Our population was stopped from rising too fast in the past mainly by disease and famine.

Diseases caught from Europeans probably killed more North American Indians than did the US Cavalry. In

BETTER HYGIENE AND SANITATION

Hygienic conditions have greatly reduced deaths among mothers and newborn babies. In particular, clean water is essential as dirty water spreads diseases. Money is needed for new equipment, such as water-treatment works, and to educate people to understand the importance of good hygiene and **sanitation**. *This village in Gambia (see right) has clean piped water which its people can collect from faucets in the street.*

NATURAL DANGERS

Humans are fairly large, strong animals. Even so, prehistoric people were probably attacked by hungry carnivores (meat-eating creatures). Humans, however, have used their intelligence and tool-making skills to invent buildings that protect them, and methods to control predators, pests, and diseases. Many children are protected by being inoculated against diseases like smallpox (see below).

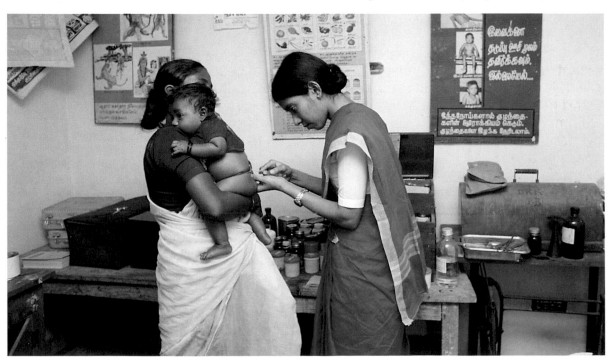

DEFICIENCY DISEASES

These are diseases caused by a lack, or deficiency, of a certain food or nutrient. They affect millions of people in poor countries. Many sufferers have several of these diseases.

● Kwashiorkor is due to lack of protein-containing foods, which normally help to build and repair body parts. It causes a "pot belly" swollen with fluid, thin arms and legs, pale crackly skin, and inability to fight off illnesses.

● Beri beri is due to lack of vitamin B1, contained in fresh green vegetables and wholemeal cereals. It causes numbness and tingling, weak muscles, confusion and heart problems.

● Rickets is due to lack of vitamin D, found in fish, eggs, and dairy products. Rickets causes weak, deformed, and brittle bones.

● Scurvy is due to lack of vitamin C, found in fresh vegetables and fruits, especially citrus fruits such as oranges. It causes coarse rough skin, stiff arms and legs, and gums and other parts that bleed at the slightest injury.

● Anemia is due to lack of the mineral iron, found in liver, dairy products, green vegetables, and many fruits. It causes paleness, tiredness, and increased risk of infections.

● Pellagra is due to lack of B2 vitamins, found in yeast, milk, meat, and green vegetables. It causes diarrhea, skin and mental disorders.

recent times cholera, typhus, and malaria have been great killers. The human population throughout the world has risen since diseases have been checked.

Famine, too, has taken its toll. Starvation is a daily event in some countries, even though there is food to spare in others. Millions of people die during famines even though the planet is capable in principle of feeding all its people, and more. There are also diseases caused by not having enough of particular sorts of food. Such diseases weaken people so much that they cannot resist other illnesses. Often these are diarrheal diseases caught by children (see page 21).

If children do not have a full and balanced diet, they do not develop properly, physically or mentally. They grow up to be adults whose physical and mental abilities are lowered. This makes it more difficult to educate people and to help them improve the way they live.

POPULATION IN EUROPE

From the middle of the 1700s, the human population has grown in numbers at a startling rate. The increase began in Europe. Why did it happen?

From around 1700, farming methods improved. Machines were invented to replace farmworkers. Open "common land" which anyone could use was steadily being enclosed by fences and hedges. Sheep and cattle were no longer allowed to roam. Fields were used in strict order, so that the plant foods stayed in the soil. More food could be grown in each area.

The improvement in roads was just as important. People moved about more easily. Foods could be taken longer distances to market, and more quickly. People's diets improved. This, in turn, helped to reduce the number of deaths, especially among babies and children. Yet the number of children being born stayed high.

THE ENCLOSURES
The maps show a village before (A) and after (B) fields became closed in. The land changed from being common land, shared among villagers, to being controlled by a few people while others worked for them. The result was that much more food was produced for sale to the towns – where most of the farm workers had gone to live.

Map A
1 church 2 rectory 3 cottages
4 common grazing land
5 grange barn to hold Lord of the Manor's share of the harvest
6 cultivated strips, one for each villager, farmed by 2-crop system

Map B
1 church 2 rectory
3 more cottages
4 grange barn has become the house of a rich Town Merchant
5 new farms
6 fields enclosed and farmed by more efficient 4-crop system
7 turnips and clover feed animals overwintering in barns

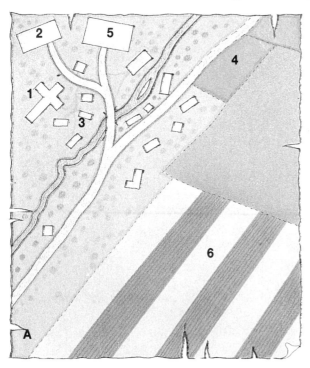

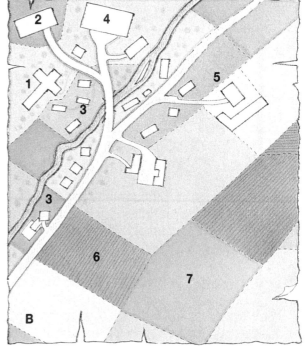

From about 1800, there were great advances in sanitation and public health. They happened in many towns and cities across Europe, and London is a good example. This city had always been a mixture of crowded, unhealthy dwellings for the poor people, and large houses in their own grounds for the rich. As the city grew through the centuries, the wealthy moved out, towards the country. Towards the center, the slums and overcrowding increased.

With the building of canals and railways came changes. Large numbers of houses were cleared for canal basins, railway tracks, engine houses, stations, and railway yards. New roads were built to carry goods and people to and from the stations. Large blocks of offices rose up, and with them came hotels and shops. This great increase in technology and trade required the building of a sewerage system.

As time went on, the railway and road systems grew rapidly within the city and around its edges. People could live away from the center and travel to work. Groups of small houses were built. Each had its own water and sanitary connections. The **suburbs** had begun. People were living cleaner, easier, better-fed lives. Fewer died from disease, poverty, overwork, or lack of food, and so the population rose.

WHAT THEY SAY
A letter written in about 1800 showed the changes brought about as the old dirt roads became firm, smooth tarmac: "A stage coach was four or five days in creeping an hundred miles … but now! a country fellow, one hundred miles from London, jumps on a coach box in the morning, and … gets to town by night."
How does this compare with travel today?

TIMES PAST
As poor people moved into the cities, poverty and deprivation increased, leading to slum conditions. William Hogarth captured the slums of London in this engraving "Night" in 1738.

PEOPLE ON THE MOVE

Throughout our history people have **migrated**. Early peoples were regularly on the move, finding new land for their flocks and fresh fields for their crops. From about the 5th century, the Goths, Vandals, and Huns moved from the North into the crumbling Roman Empire. In the 13th century, the Mongols swept into Eastern Europe from Asia. Britain was colonized by successive

WAR LOSSES
● Probably some 10 million people from Europe, or of European descent, died in World War I (1914-18).
● In World War II (1939-45), this number was probably more than 20 million.
● Wars continue in several regions. In the Iran–Iraq conflict of the 1980s, there were more than a million deaths.

EUROPE SLOWS, AMERICA SPEEDS
This chart shows the relative growths of the populations of North America and Europe. The numbers of people in Europe have continued to rise, but the rate of increase is gradually slowing. The rise in America has been fast.

Europe (%)

North America (%)

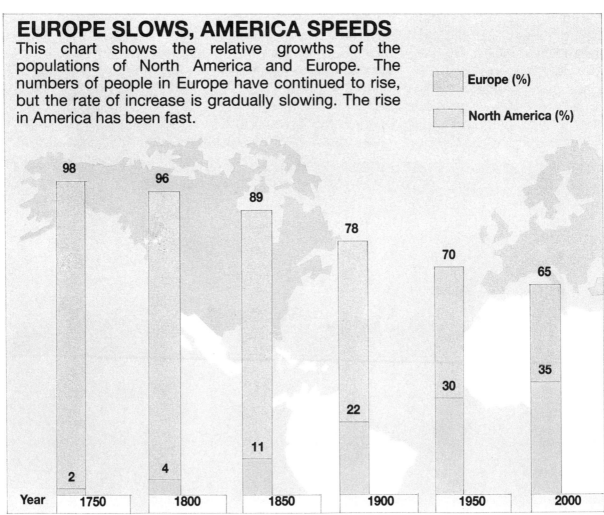

| Year | 1750 | 1800 | 1850 | 1900 | 1950 | 2000 |

Europe: 98, 96, 89, 78, 70, 65
North America: 2, 4, 11, 22, 30, 35

waves of Celts, Saxons, Vikings, and Normans. Africa has been settled by people from the North.

In recent times the largest movements of people have involved Europeans. They have settled all over the world. In Africa, the Americas, and Australia, many of the people already living there have been over-whelmed by European invasions. At first, explorers went to these far-off lands to satisfy their curiosity, then to find materials for trade, and later to settle.

In spite of better health and feeding, there was still hardship and poverty. In 1840, the potato famines in Ireland and Germany killed thousands. Common land was taken away from people, and the Industrial Revolution meant that machinery began to take the place of workers. If they could not find jobs in the new towns and cities, people suffered. This caused waves of migration. Some 37 million people moved to the United States from Europe between 1820 and 1980, hoping for prosperity and a freer life. Most migrated before World War II. Similarly, Spanish-speaking people from Europe have moved to Central and South America.

FORCED MIGRATIONS

- 20 million people were brought to the Americas between the 16th and 20th centuries.
- 150,000 convicts were sent from Europe to Australia as early settlers in the 18th and 19th centuries.
- Up to eight million people were forced to move by the Nazis before and during World War II, and many were enslaved.
- Some one million Russians were forced to go to Siberia in the 19th century.
- During the partitioning of the Indian continent into India and Pakistan, 14 million people have had to move.
- 10 million fled from war in East Pakistan (now Bangladesh) in the 1960-70s.
- War has driven many people from Vietnam, Cuba, Israel, and other countries.
- In 1980, some 10 million people around the world were still not settled.

THE BOAT PEOPLE
After the war in Vietnam, many refugees fled to other countries, risking their lives in small boats on the open seas.

DEVELOPING NATIONS

Since the end of World War II, the peoples of Africa, Asia, and South America have increased by 2 billion. They have doubled their numbers. Their story over the past 50 years is the same as Europe's about 200 years ago. The death rate has dropped sharply, especially among mothers and their babies and young children. The length of time that a person can expect to live has also increased.

The death rates have been lowered by better food

THE BIRTH POTENTIAL
These are two population pyramids for the developing countries and industrialized countries. The dark colors with outlines show the age groups in 1985. The light colors are estimates for them in 2025, 40 years later. The extra numbers of children surviving will grow into adults, who will live longer, and in turn have yet more children. This is called the birth potential.

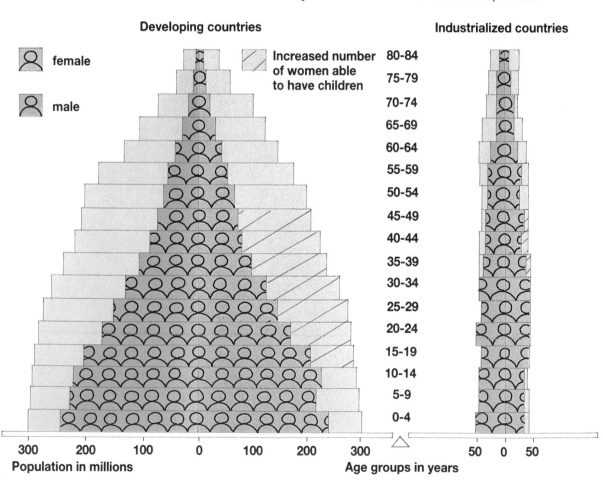

and general health. Farmers in many places have learned to grow better harvests. They use improved animal and plant breeds and more fertilizers. In times of famine, and in places where food is always short, international aid may come to the rescue.

The lives of mothers and their babies have been saved by using simple methods of avoiding disease. The biggest killer of infants is diarrhea, caused by a number of different diseases. Babies, especially, die from loss of water and vital minerals and nutrients from their bodies. By learning simple health measures, mothers can avoid this. The use of boiled water and clean clothes at the birth of a baby also saves lives.

These habits are taught by health workers who are trained with the money from international aid. They work in villages and towns. Other programs organized in this way have helped to develop clean water supplies and proper sanitation.

Lower death rates mean that more people grow up to have children. They live longer, too, so this may increase the number of children they can raise. This is a major part of the world population explosion.

KILLER DIARRHEA

Diarrhea kills hundreds of children daily, particularly in the poor countries of South America, Africa, and Asia. Yet simple measures can help prevent the problem:
● Use only clean or boiled water for drinking, cooking, and washing.
● Wash hands after using the toilet.
● Wash hands before preparing, cooking, or eating food.
● Peel or wash fresh food thoroughly.

THE DIARRHEA DISEASE CYCLE

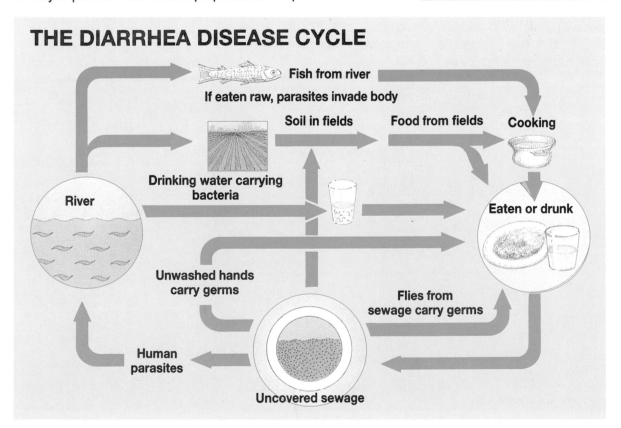

Fish from river
If eaten raw, parasites invade body
Soil in fields
Food from fields
Cooking
Drinking water carrying bacteria
River
Eaten or drunk
Unwashed hands carry germs
Flies from sewage carry germs
Human parasites
Uncovered sewage

FROM COUNTRY TO CITY

People usually move for a purpose. When they reach their chosen place, they tend to settle and try to make a home. They may move huge distances or simply from country to town.

The movement from country to town has happened throughout history, but it has now greatly increased. It happened to European cities in the last two centuries. This was a slow process compared to the movements in developing countries today.

The cities of developing countries are expanding fast. In 1950, there were twice as many people in the cities of industrialized countries as there were in the cities of poorer countries. Now it is almost the reverse. "Megacities" with over five million people in them are developing, with cities in Central and South America showing the greatest growth. Mexico City is approaching 20 million.

MOVING TO THE CITIES

● By the year 2000, about 17% of the world's people will live in cities of five million or more.
● By the same year, there will probably be twice as many cities of more than one million people in industrialized countries than there were in 1950.
● There will be probably seven times as many such cities in poorer countries as there were in 1950.
● On average, the number of children that each woman has is lower in cities than in rural areas.

POLLUTION

Besides overcrowding and homelessness, there is pollution in large cities. Waste, sewage, and car exhaust gases are growing problems in all cities (see below).

The dreams of country-dwellers, as they set off to the city, do not always come true. The World Resources Institute reports that "an estimated two-fifths of the urban population in less developed countries lives in slum and squatter areas..." Other people have no home at all and live on the city streets. Toilets and water taps are shared among many people.

ONE CITY OR SEVERAL TOWNS?

There are few advantages to having one giant city with almost deserted lands around it. A more sensible solution would be a network of towns, bringing their advantages closer to more people.

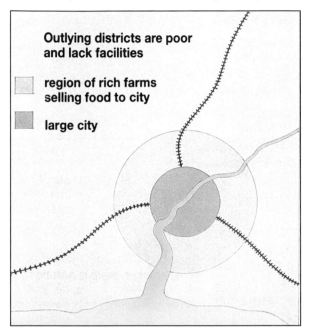

Outlying districts are poor and lack facilities

☐ **region of rich farms selling food to city**

☐ **large city**

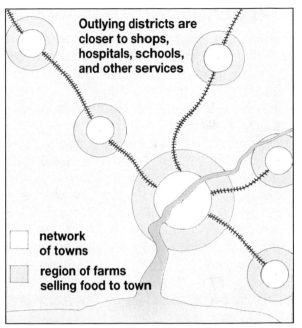

Outlying districts are closer to shops, hospitals, schools, and other services

☐ **network of towns**

☐ **region of farms selling food to town**

THE LURE OF THE BIG CITY

There are many reasons why people migrate from country to town. They may have no choice. Laws are used to drive peasant farmers from their land, as has happened in the past in Brazil. It is taking place today in some Asian countries. Droughts and famines may also force people to move and find food.

Other people expect to find work in the city, and a better life for their children. There are often schools, hospitals, entertainment, and shops which are not found in rural areas. Young people who find work in cities can send money home to help their families. Often, however, reality is very different and the immigrants end up homeless and sleeping on the streets (see left).

PLANNING POPULATIONS

The populations of developed countries are growing more slowly, mainly due to family planning. This is probably because people calculate that a large family means less for each child and a harder life for parents. However, these countries only account for one-fifth of the world's population.

More important is what is happening in developing countries. Here, religions or cultural traditions may forbid family planning. Some governments do nothing to encourage smaller families. Some people want a large family, while others are forced to have many children.

So what is happening in developing countries around the world? The picture is mixed. For example, the Chinese people have rapidly reduced the size of their families. In Kenya, family size has remained high. In Bolivia, it has fallen very slightly. Government efforts to

THE EXTENDED FAMILY
In many developing countries, as here in Bangladesh, a household usually consists of grandparents, parents, and several children.

encourage smaller families in these three countries are very different. China has had a campaign that makes people lose money if they have more than one child. In Kenya, some effort has been made to encourage people to have fewer children, but with little success. In Bolivia, the government does almost nothing.

On average, the number of children each woman has in her lifetime (her fertility) does seem to be falling. But more could be done. The UN Children's Fund, UNICEF, has estimated that one-third of pregnant women in poorer countries do not want any more children. Yet most have no knowledge or means of family planning.

PREVENTING PREGNANCY

Family planning allows people to choose when they have babies.
● Almost 75% of married women in developed countries carry out family planning by using **contraceptives**.
● In poorer countries the average is just over 50% of women. In some African countries the average is only 10%.

In 1967, 30 world governments signed a United Nations Declaration on Population. They believed in the need for family planning. These were the UN's reasons:
● The population problem can spoil efforts to improve standards of living.
● Most parents want to know how to plan their families.
● To be able to plan a family is seen as a basic human right.
● Lasting peace on Earth depends on managing population growth.
● Family planning helps each person achieve full growth in every sense, including an individual's freedom and rights.

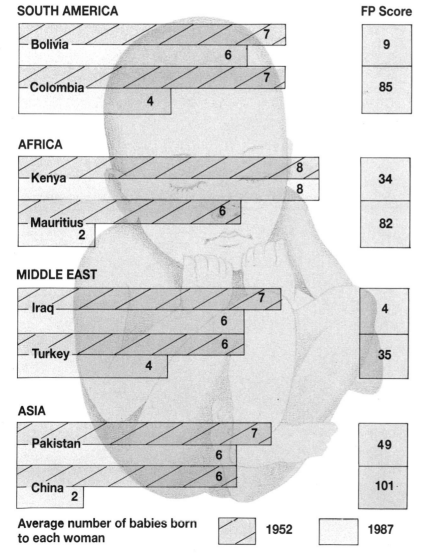

SOUTH AMERICA — **FP Score**

	1952	1987	FP Score
Bolivia	7	6	9
Colombia	7	4	85

AFRICA

	1952	1987	FP Score
Kenya	8	8	34
Mauritius	6	2	82

MIDDLE EAST

	1952	1987	FP Score
Iraq	7	6	4
Turkey	6	4	35

ASIA

	1952	1987	FP Score
Pakistan	7	6	49
China	6	2	101

Average number of babies born to each woman   ⬜ 1952   ⬜ 1987

HAPPY FAMILIES?
This chart shows how the average number of babies born to each mother has changed over 35 years, for various countries. The FP Score is a measure of the effort that country has put into family planning. A very high score means that much time, money and effort is being spent. A low score, below about 25, indicates that hardly anything is being done. Compare the various figures. Is a high FP Score linked to a fall in the birth rate?

THE FAMILY

Part of our escape from the People Trap involves a fall in family size. Many women or couples want to have smaller families – but they cannot, for various reasons.

Children can earn money and help the family income. In Java, Southeast Asia, a seven-year-old boy may start work by looking after the family's chickens and ducks. His responsibilities increase with age. By the age of 15 he has earned enough to repay all his keep over the years, such as his food, clothes, and bedding. In Tanzania, Africa, girls between five and nine years of

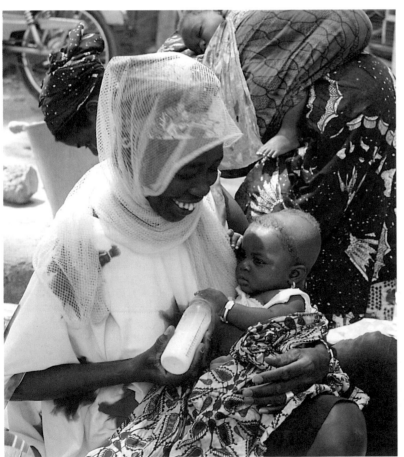

KEEPING UP FAMILY SIZE
In a number of African countries, bottle feeding with milk made from dried powder is encouraged instead of natural breast feeding. At first the milk is cheap, but later in a baby's life it becomes very expensive. By then breast feeding is difficult to start. There is little clean water and equipment to sterilize bottles, so many babies suffer. Death rates are high.

NO FIFTH BIRTHDAY

Babies and young children, along with elderly people, are those most at risk from hunger and disease. The table shows how many children die before the age of five. Look up the countries on a map. Where are most of them situated? Most deaths occur before the age of one, so some parents have a lot of children in case some die.

Number of children per 100 who died before reaching 5 in 1987

Niger	Angola	Mozambique	Somalia	Ethiopia	Guinea	Malawi	Sierra Leone	Mali	Afghanistan
24	24	25	26	26	26	27	30	30	33

age may spend an average of three-and-a-half hours each day working in the home. In cities such as Sao Paulo, Brazil, children sell newspapers or run errands for office workers.

Often a woman has no choice but to have many children. Living far from a town, religious beliefs, or lack of education can prevent her from using the family planning services, even if they are available.

Some cultures look with favor on large families. It is part of their tradition. In countries such as Kenya and Zimbabwe, women consider themselves successful if they have lots of children.

Children have always been an "insurance policy" for their parents' future. They will help to care for their parents in old age – or at least, they should. As times change, these old traditions are not always followed.

CHILDREN AT WORK

In many countries, children cannot go to school because they must work. They herd animals, they plant and harvest crops, and they clean the house and cook food. Some, like this small boy, are employed in factories and work shops. The importance of child labor may drop in the future as more children have to go to school and more people earn sufficient money to keep a family.

A NATURAL CONTROL?

WHAT THEY SAY

Thomas Malthus' book on population growth was the source of many debates. In it, he states: "Population, when unchecked, increases in a geometrical ratio. Subsistence only increases in an arithmetic ratio." In 1803 he published a second version. In this he added other factors that might control our population, such as marrying and having children later in life. His thinking has influenced many people over the years.

The Englishman Thomas Robert Malthus was born in 1766. He became a clergyman, **economist**, and mathematician. He wrote about human population in his Essay on Population (1798). The English naturalists Charles Darwin and Alfred Wallace used his ideas to form their theory of **evolution**. The effects of Malthus' views can still be seen today in writings about our present situation.

Malthus said that we would always produce a population which was too big for the food supplies and the other things we need to survive. He said that,

CHARLES DARWIN
Darwin sailed around the world in 1831-36 on the ship Beagle, *studying animals, plants, rocks, and fossils. Later he published a famous book about evolution,* On The Origin of Species *(1859). Evolution was very controversial at the time, and Darwin was influenced by the writings of Malthus. He saw that in nature most animals and plants produced far more offspring than can possibly survive. Therefore, many of the offspring were bound to die.*

as a result, there would always be the three "evils" of war, famine, and disease. These would bring our numbers within the bounds of the supplies available.

Today, some people follow Malthus' argument. Their view is that we do not have a population problem because we will never be able to overcome war, famine, and disease. These disasters will always reduce the world population. They will control our numbers.

One problem with views based on those of Malthus is that they are "self-fulfilling." If we believe them, they will happen. If we think that famine, disease, and war will always be with us, and do nothing about them, then they will always be with us.

Other people argue that a population even higher than the one on Earth today can live in comfort on the planet. In principle, they say, there can be enough food, water, and fuel for everyone. Also, if resources were shared more fairly, standards of living could rise for all the people in the world.

IS NOTHING INEVITABLE?

- Just because our numbers have risen during the two or three million years of our existence, it does not mean that they must rise for ever.
- Sometime in the future the population rocket might level off as it has done in the past.
- It is important to remember that Malthus was writing at a time when the population in Europe was shooting up.
- Since then Europe's population has begun to level off.

CHILD BEGGARS
Poverty is a constant threat for many large families in poorer countries. Often children are sent out to beg for money on the streets because people are more likely to take pity on a begging child than on an adult.

THE DEBT CRISIS

Education, food **subsidies**, and family planning all cost money. Governments must spend money to train and employ teachers and health workers, and to provide education and supplies for family planning.

Does enough aid go from rich, industrialized countries to the poorer countries to achieve these things? The fact is that, overall, more money is paid by developing countries to rich countries, in the form of repayments on debts and loans, than goes in the opposite direction as international aid.

Tanzania, in Africa, is a typical example. Each year the country must pay enormous sums to settle debts with the big banks of developed countries. These amounts are nine times the money that the country can earn from its exports, mainly copper. To repay its debts, Tanzania must borrow yet more money.

Since the early 1980s, some poor countries have

WHAT THEY SAY

"The recent destruction of much of Africa's dryland agricultural production was more severe than if an invading army had pursued a 'scorched earth' policy. Yet most of the affected governments still spend far more to protect their people from invading armies than from the invading desert."
The United Nations World Commission on Environment and Development Report, 1987.

THE EDUCATION TRAP

It is essential that the standard of education be raised in developing countries. In remote, poverty stricken areas like this in Bolivia (see below), people are struggling in very difficult conditions to educate their children.

demanded changes in how they repay their debts. The International Monetary Fund (IMF), run by big banks and governments of industrialized countries, has arranged for easier repayments. In return, it has insisted that the debtor countries spend less on their own public programs, such as health, education, and food subsidies. This has meant that the debtor countries produce more, but earn less. People work longer, for less money, and suffer poorer health. For example in Peru, a woman must work seven times longer than she did in 1981 to earn enough money to buy a pound of rice. In Brazil, the infant death rate rose by one-fifth between 1982 and 1986, probably because underfed mothers gave birth to underweight babies. Some banks have "written off" debts as they could not be reclaimed. They have taken huge losses.

MONEY FOR THE MILITARY

Some governments of developing countries spend their money on arms and armies, often to control their own people. In Ethiopia, millions are hungry, while the government fights a civil war. The arms makers in industrialized countries get profits from the sale of weapons to poorer countries.

NEVER-ENDING DEBT

South American countries have more than doubled their exports of goods between 1980 and 1985. Yet their earnings from those exports fell by 5% each year. They were "running backwards." This table shows by how much a country's debt outweighs what it can earn in exports.

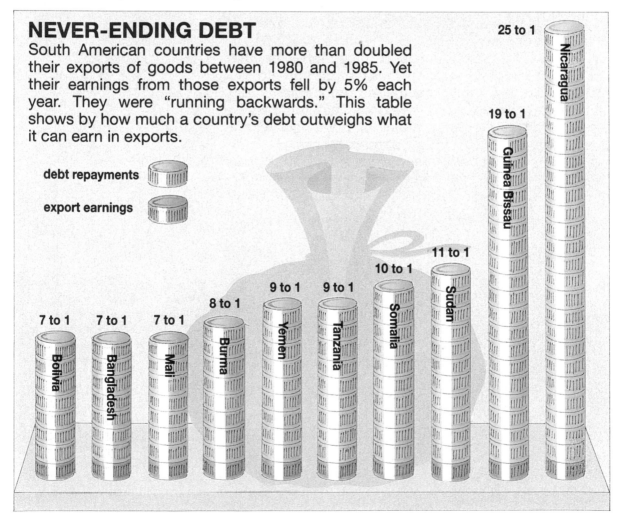

debt repayments

export earnings

25 to 1 — Nicaragua
19 to 1 — Guinea Bissau
11 to 1 — Sudan
10 to 1 — Somalia
9 to 1 — Tanzania
9 to 1 — Yemen
8 to 1 — Burma
7 to 1 — Mali
7 to 1 — Bangladesh
7 to 1 — Bolivia

PEOPLE AND POLLUTION

A major factor in the population problem is that people cause pollution. As the human population increases, more food must be grown, and more goods are made. If farming and industry continue as they are today, more pollution will be produced. The answer is not only to control our population growth, but also to change farming methods and industrial technology, so that they cause less pollution.

Some of the most dangerous pollutants come from producing energy. For example, power plants around the world burn vast quantities of coal. Coal produces **greenhouse gases** which will warm up the world in years to come. Burning coal also produces **acid rain**, which kills trees and life in rivers and lakes. Aspects of modern living that cause this sort of pollution cannot go on forever. Most of the technology in use today wastes too much energy and causes too much pollution. However, even if we change to the least-polluting methods, we cannot increase our numbers for ever.

ENERGY RESERVES AND USE

*World energy resources, like world energy use, is very unevenly distributed. The diagram on the right illustrates the production of the **fossil fuels** coal, oil, and natural gas in the world and the use of hydropower and fuelwood. The energy value of the fuels is given in million tons of oil equivalent (OE) so that they can be compared.*

Most of the industrialized countries use fossil fuels to fulfil their energy needs. Many developing countries, which have few fossil fuel reserves, rely more on renewable energy forms such as hydropower, solar energy, and firewood. It is essential that all countries develop alternative energy sources and cut down on energy consumption if we are to supply the increasing energy needs and lower pollution.

The amount of energy used in one year by each person is given in joules, which is a measure of the capacity to do work. Developed nations use about 80% of world energy, but they make up only 25% of the world's population. North America has the highest energy use and Asia the lowest.

HELPING MOTHER EARTH

Wind turbines like these near Palm Springs in California (see right) are being used to produce pollution-free energy. In Denmark local groups can have government help in building a wind generator of their own. Any electricity that they do not need can be sold to the government.

LIMITING OURSELVES

A United Nations forecast suggests that the human population might level off at 10 billion around 2100 AD if fertility rates continue to fall. Can we wait that long? We must act now to cut down the pollution produced by power plants (see left) and factories.

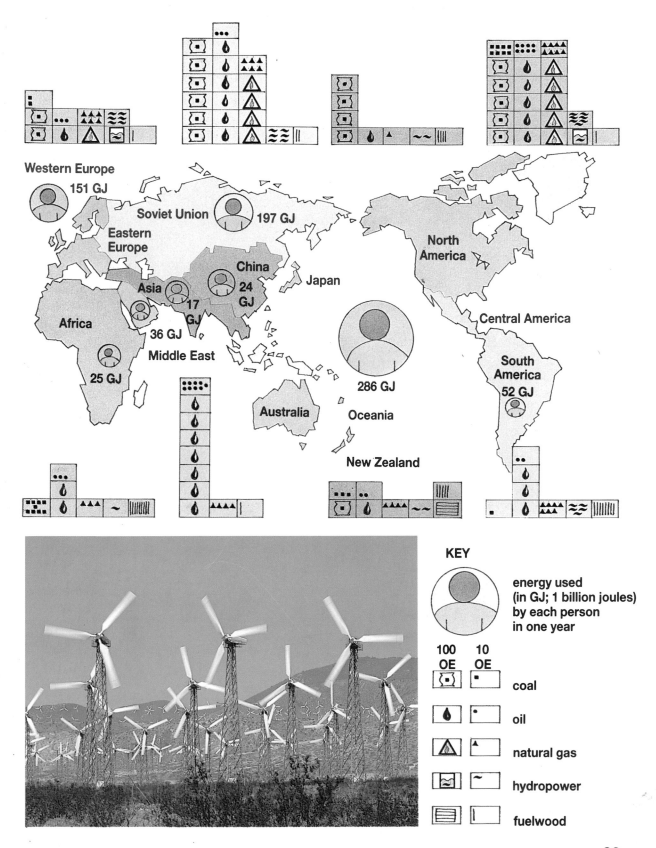

Western Europe
151 GJ

Soviet Union
197 GJ

Eastern
Europe

China
24 GJ

Asia
17 GJ

36 GJ
Middle East

Africa
25 GJ

North
America

Central America

South
America
52 GJ

Japan

Australia

Oceania

New Zealand

286 GJ

KEY

energy used
(in GJ; 1 billion joules)
by each person
in one year

100 OE	10 OE	
[coal icon]	[coal icon]	coal
[oil icon]	[oil icon]	oil
[gas icon]	[gas icon]	natural gas
[hydro icon]	[hydro icon]	hydropower
[fuelwood icon]	[fuelwood icon]	fuelwood

FEEDING THE WORLD

In the 1960s, the "Green Revolution" began. This is the name given to a number of changes in farming that happened during that time. Plant breeders developed new forms of wheat and rice which took up fertilizers more readily, resisted disease, grew faster, and gave better yields. In many places, two crops could be grown each year instead of one. At first, the question of whether we could grow enough food for our rising population seemed to have been answered.

FISH WITH RICE

Farmers in Thailand have recently gone back to "rice-fish" farming that produces little pollution, and works with nature rather than against it. The idea is to raise fish in the flooded paddy fields where rice grows. This used to happen many years ago, but chemical fertilizers, pesticides, modern farming techniques, and irrigation programs all did away with the fish. Now farmers are going back to the old methods, while improving them still further.

Fish caught to provide food for the family or to sell

Flooded paddy fields where rice plants grow in the wet season

Fish droppings spread manure evenly across paddy fields

Fish feed on weeds and pest insects in the water that would otherwise damage the rice crop, as well as on household scraps and unwanted bits of the plants

Nursery pond to protect baby fish from predators

Deep pond where a few fish can survive in the dry season

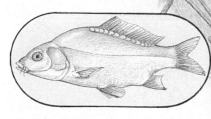

Fish raised include tilapia, silver barb, and common carp

Raised banks stabilized and planted with crops such as corn,

sugar cane, beans, papaya, bananas

Today, there is enough food for nearly a billion people more than are alive on Earth. Yet 950 million people do not have enough food to do a day's work. Millions die from starvation each year. Reasons for this situation vary in different parts of the world. The Green Revolution helped mainly those countries that used wheat or rice for their basic food, chiefly in Asia, Australasia, Europe, and North America. European countries, the US, and Canada export wheat.

Countries in Africa mostly use root crops for their basic diet. Their harvests have improved only slowly, while their populations have climbed rapidly. African countries are the most in need of aid, especially war-torn Ethiopia and the drought-ridden Sahel region.

Across the whole world, feeding standards have slowly risen in recent years. Whether they will continue to rise is uncertain. The new, intensive ways of farming are causing soils to become worn out and **eroded** away. Organic farming, in which natural fertilizers rather than chemical ones are used, is better for the soil and protects it for longer. Carried out properly, it is also cheaper. Farmers are beginning to change their ways.

PROFIT OUT OF SUBSIDY

In some places the effects of the Green Revolution have been reduced.

● One reason is that in order to grow Green Revolution crops, the improved types of seeds must be bought each year, together with fertilizer. For peasant farmers in poorer countries, these seeds and fertilizers may be too expensive.

● One reason why the farmers cannot afford the seeds is that world prices of wheat and rice have dropped a great deal, and the farmers' harvests have brought them less profit.

● One reason why prices have fallen is that the governments of developed countries pay their farmers some of the cost of growing wheat. Such payments are called subsidies.

● Because of the subsidies, the farmers in developed countries can sell their wheat at low prices. This keeps down the profits of the farmers in poorer countries.

● In both developing and industrialized countries, soils become less fertile and water is poisoned.

ANIMAL POWER
Many farmers in developing countries cannot afford to buy or run expensive tractors. They use traditional animals, like these water buffalo in Thailand, to plough their fields.

SCIENCE – A SAVIOR?

Can science find the answers to the population puzzle? Certainly human beings have been very clever in using science. Starting with stone tools, the list of human inventions seems endless.

In the last two centuries, life has changed at an ever-increasing pace. The microscope and other inventions

WHAT THEY SAY

"Rapid economic growth in developing countries is essential; and they can grow more rapidly in a buoyant world economy that bolsters trade opportunities."
Sir Shridath Ramphal, Secretary-General of the British Commonwealth.

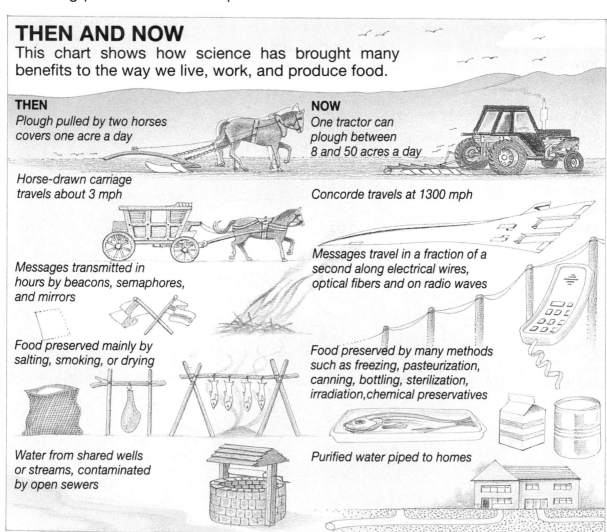

THEN AND NOW

This chart shows how science has brought many benefits to the way we live, work, and produce food.

THEN
Plough pulled by two horses covers one acre a day

NOW
One tractor can plough between 8 and 50 acres a day

Horse-drawn carriage travels about 3 mph

Concorde travels at 1300 mph

Messages transmitted in hours by beacons, semaphores, and mirrors

Messages travel in a fraction of a second along electrical wires, optical fibers and on radio waves

Food preserved mainly by salting, smoking, or drying

Food preserved by many methods such as freezing, pasteurization, canning, bottling, sterilization, irradiation, chemical preservatives

Water from shared wells or streams, contaminated by open sewers

Purified water piped to homes

have helped us to understand our bodies and to find methods of family planning and birth control. Science has helped us to change the way that plants and animals grow, as part of the Green Revolution (see page 34), so that there is more food available. Medicine has also helped, with improved surgical techniques, drugs, and preventative medicine such as the development of vaccines for treating childhood diseases.

There are further scientific wonders to come in tomorrow's world. For example, body-building protein food for people can be made from crude oil. Very powerful computers will help us make better predictions of weather and climate. Improved engineering techniques and new inventions will provide us with alternative sources of energy powered by the wind, tides, and Sun, and at much lower prices than energy can be made by coal and nuclear power today.

However, science is a double-edged sword. It has draw-backs as well as benefits, as explained on page 38.

GENETIC ENGINEERING

This area of science concerns altering the **genes** in a living thing. The genes hold the "blueprint for life." They are instructions, in the form of the chemical code known as DNA, for building and maintaining that living thing. Alter the genes, and the plant or animal grows and works differently. Genetic engineering has enabled scientists to make new drugs and other advances in medicine.

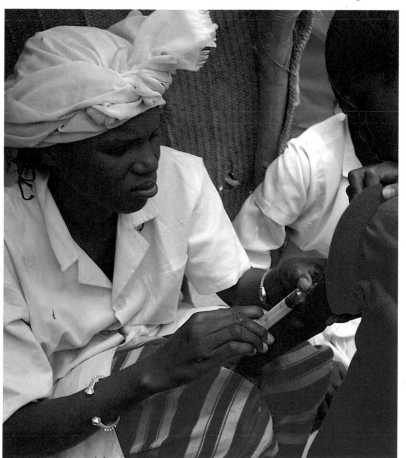

SAVING LIFE
Advances in medical science have saved millions of lives. However, many children in developing countries still die from childhood infections. Vaccination programs, like this one in Mali, Africa against meningitis, should help reduce childhood mortality.

OR A CURSE?

Many scientific discoveries will help reduce the levels of pollution we have today. Many others, however, have the potential to make matters worse.

The natural world is an intricate and delicately-balanced web of living things. Wherever we humans step in, the balance is usually upset. We spray crops and treat animals with many different chemicals. However, many of these chemicals are dangerous.

For example, DDT and dieldrin kill insect pests. But now they are banned in developed countries because they also threaten birds and mammals. They are also believed to be poisonous even to the people whose food supply they are supposed to protect.

DDT AND FOOD CHAINS
DDT, used to control insect pests of crops, affected many insects. The insects were eaten by birds, and the DDT-affected crops were also eaten. The DDT built up in the bodies of these animals, poisoning them. DDT also entered the water cycle, contaminating the food chains of fish and other water animals. It has been found in penguins in the Antarctic.

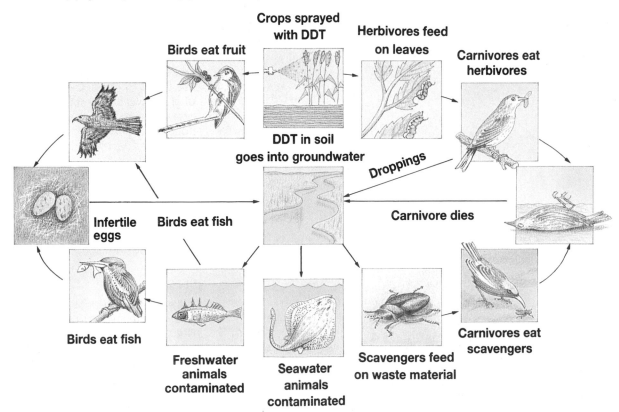

Birds eat fruit

Crops sprayed with DDT

Herbivores feed on leaves

Carnivores eat herbivores

DDT in soil goes into groundwater

Droppings

Carnivore dies

Infertile eggs

Birds eat fish

Carnivores eat scavengers

Birds eat fish

Freshwater animals contaminated

Seawater animals contaminated

Scavengers feed on waste material

SAVES CROPS, BUT KILLS BIRDS
Large fields of crops, like this wheat field in Britain, are prone to attack by pests. Unfortunately, the chemicals used to attack the pests often have other effects as well. For example, the pesticide dieldrin can no longer be used in Britain. It protected the crops from insect attack, but it also killed many birds, and it has collected in the bodies of many other animals.

WHAT THEY SAY

The United Nations World Commission on Environment and Development suggested in 1987 that our modern way of life is too energy-expensive. It said that for the poor developing countries to become developed, like the rich countries in Europe and North America, we would need five times as much energy as we use today. However, the threats of global warming and acid rain probably rule out even a doubling of energy use, especially if we continue to use fossil fuels. We cannot go on wasting energy as we have done in the past. We are relying too much on coal and oil, and so damaging our world with acid rain and greenhouse gases.

Although we shall never be able to do without science and technology, they cannot supply all the answers. We must learn to live more in harmony with the natural world if our descendants are to have a chance of surviving in it.

KILLING PESTS
Spraying with pesticides is used throughout the world to control insect pests. Here in Zambia they are spraying chemicals to control tsetse flies, which can transmit sleeping sickness. Unfortunately, no pesticide treatment is absolutely safe.

LIVING WITHIN LIMITS

There are at least three ways of viewing our present plight on Earth. People who argue as Malthus did say we can do nothing about population growth. We just have to suffer. Some scientists would say that we can solve any problems that came along using new inventions and technology. So there is no need for concern. A third view is that the Earth can put up with so much, but no more. There are limits, and if we go beyond those limits, we threaten all living things.

GOVERNMENT AID

Many governments have developed population-control programs but these have not always been successful. In many cases people had little choice.

● Some governments such as Japan have tried to reduce the birth rate in their country by using education and improving living standards. The people have been given the chance to make a choice.

● Other governments have used various degrees of force and enticement. Some Eastern European countries offered free abortion, but then withdrew it when too many women used it.

● Governments such as in India began a sterilization program for men. Although partly successful, it led to some less-educated men being bullied. It has now stopped.

● Some governments control family size directly, by law. In China, laws were introduced that meant families with more than one child had to pay fines.

The only sure way of solving the People Trap is to improve the standard of living and education of all the people of the world so that they can accept the need to limit the size of their family.

HEALTH CARE

Most developed countries have effective health care for both adults and children. It is essential that such care be made available in all countries. Here in Kenya, traveling clinics visit villages to give advice and check on the health and development of their patients.

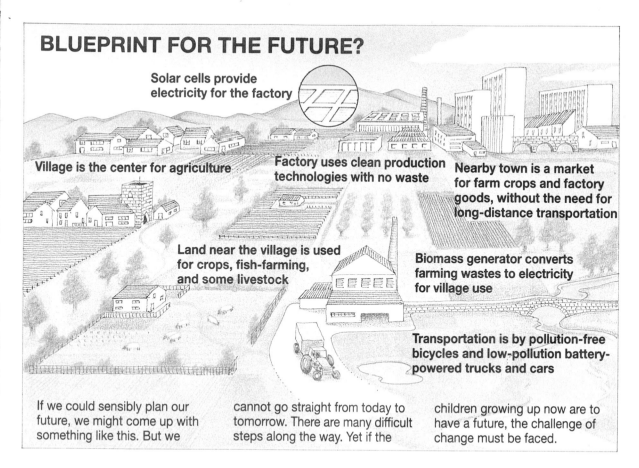

BLUEPRINT FOR THE FUTURE?

Solar cells provide electricity for the factory

Village is the center for agriculture

Factory uses clean production technologies with no waste

Nearby town is a market for farm crops and factory goods, without the need for long-distance transportation

Land near the village is used for crops, fish-farming, and some livestock

Biomass generator converts farming wastes to electricity for village use

Transportation is by pollution-free bicycles and low-pollution battery-powered trucks and cars

If we could sensibly plan our future, we might come up with something like this. But we cannot go straight from today to tomorrow. There are many difficult steps along the way. Yet if the children growing up now are to have a future, the challenge of change must be faced.

The limits are many and varied. We can only release so much polluting gas into the air, and spray so many chemicals onto the land, and pump so much waste into rivers and seas. The air, land, and water can only absorb a certain amount of pollution. There are also limits to all the things we use. Iron, tin, copper, oil, and many more useful materials will run out in the future, unless we cut down on using them. There are also limits to our water and food supplies.

The more people there are on Earth, the more quickly all our resources are likely to be used up. The answer must be to try to live within the limits of nature. People will have to use less of the Earth's resources, mainly in developed countries where more than two-thirds of the world's raw materials are used by only one-fifth of its population. These aims recognize that we need science and technology. For humans to be successful in the future will mean two main things: fairer distribution of natural resources coupled with population control by widespread use of family planning.

WHAT THEY SAY

"There will be no day or days when a new world order comes into being. Step by step and here and there it will arrive, and, even as it comes into being it will develop fresh perspectives, discover unsuspected problems, and go on to new adventures." *H. G. Wells, author of science-fiction books such as The Time Machine and War of the Worlds, in 1942.*

WHAT TO DO TO HELP

Controlling the size of world population is a very difficult topic. It involves controlling family size, and governments and religions around the world have very different views about that. In addition, your own most powerful emotions and desires are involved. However, people should be able to consider all sides of the question before deciding the family size they want. In order to make such decisions, they need to know all the facts. Education is an important key to understanding the effect of an increasing population on the world.

Similarly, there are many things that people can do to help avoid millions of children growing up threatened by starvation and disease. Even the smallest action by an individual can help to solve the problems caused by people using too much energy, producing too much waste and pollution, and asking more of the Earth than it can give. It is up to us all to make tomorrow's world one in which everyone has enough food, reasonable education, effective health care, and safe, hygienic living conditions.

GET INVOLVED

● Join an organization like Save the Children that helps children in poorer countries to have healthier lives and better education. This will help to save children's lives and encourage people to have smaller families

● Encourage your school to help raise money to send a child in a developing country to school

● Support those trying to reduce the arms trade, especially to poorer countries. Write to your political representative asking him or her not to support governments that buy arms when their people need food, clean water, and better education

REDUCE POLLUTION

The waste and poisons created by industry will affect the death rates of all future children and encourage people to keep the birth rate high. We are all responsible and should try to cut down on pollution

● Cars are one of the biggest polluters in the world.

● Use lead-free gas if possible

● Use public transportation whenever possible

● Share your car on trips to school and work

● Use a bicycle or walk for short trips

● Help raise funds for environmental projects and people overseas by sponsored events or collections

SAVE ENERGY

If people in developed countries cut down on the energy they used, it would cut down on pollution and allow developing countries to use more energy to improve their standard of living. There are many things you can do.

● Insulate your home so that you use less fuel to keep it warm

● When you or your parents buy electrical goods, check that they are the most energy efficient ones available

● Turn off all electrical equipment when it is not in use. Do not leave lights on

LEARN FROM OTHERS

● Listen carefully to what people have to say about family life both at home and in other countries

● Learn as much as you can about the way a human life is started; what is needed for the safe growth and birth of a baby and for full growth to adulthood

● Learn about the ways to control family size, with and without using contraceptives

● Read books and watch television programs to find out how families and children live in developing countries

BUSINESS

● Invest in businesses in developing countries and those using modern technology that does not involve production of atmospheric pollutants

● Do not buy goods from companies that pay their workers starvation wages

● Sponser education and self-help groups in developing countries

IN THE SHOPS

● Be aware of the effects of what you buy. Cheap goods nearly always mean poor wages for someone

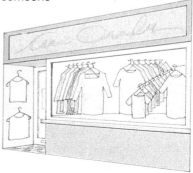

● Try to use shops that sell environment friendly products, even if they are a little more expensive

● Buy goods made of recycled material and refuse excess packaging like plastic and paper bags

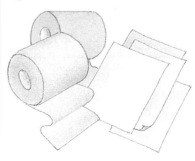

GLOSSARY

Acid rain Rain, dew, or snow that is more acidic than is usual. Acid rain is produced by the sulfur dioxide and nitrogen oxides that are given off when fossil fuels are burnt.

Biomass The mass of organic material produced as a result of life. We can use this word, for example, for all wood produced by trees or the wastes produced by animals, and even for the organic matter in the animals themselves.

Birth rate The number of animals born each year compared with their total population.

Breeding rate The number of offspring that an animal gives birth to each year.

Census The counting of a population. In developed countries a census form is sent to each house. The name, age, sex, occupation, and other information must be put on the form for everyone living in the house.

Civilization The social organization of humans. Our history shows the rise and fall of many civilizations, for example the Chinese, Egyptian, Aztec, Greek, and Roman empires.

Contraceptive An artificial means for preventing pregnancy.

Death rate The number of animals that die each year compared with their total population.

Demographer A person who measures and studies human populations by counting births, deaths, and many other things we learn about the populations of countries.

Economist A person who measures production and distribution of wealth, and proposes ways of improving them.

Eroded If land is not properly managed, for example by overgrazing of poor pasture by cattle or goats, or by overcultivation, the topsoil may be blown or washed away by the weather – it has been eroded.

Evolution The idea that living things, machines, and societies can develop and change with time. Darwin and Wallace wrote books about human and animal evolution.

Fossil fuels Coal, oil, and gas are all fossil fuels. They are all made of carbon, and if you burn them you get carbon dioxide (a greenhouse gas) and the gases that produce acid rain.

Genes Each cell of the body of a living thing has an identical set of genes. These dictate the way cells grow and behave, and are passed from one generation to the next.

Greenhouse gases Carbon dioxide, methane, nitrous oxide, and CFCs (chlorofluorocarbons) are the main greenhouse gases. They trap heat in the atmosphere, causing global warming. Most greenhouse gases are formed when fossil fuels are burnt, others are produced from manufactured goods and chemicals (see *Air Scare* in this series).

Irrigation The use of channels, trickle pipes, or sprays to feed plants with water.

Migrate Animals migrate or move from one country or district to another to live. For example, salmon migrate from river to sea, and from sea to river.

Sanitation Practical ways, for example adequate sewage disposal and clean water supplies, for improving health conditions. Good sanitation such as safe sewage disposal reduces infections and the spread of diseases.

Suburbs The outlying districts of a city.

Subsidies Money grants given by governments to farmers to encourage them to grow certain crops.